MW01274185

KIDS' STUFF

RUTH MAE RODDY

© 1996 Dramaline Publications

All Rights Reserved

Printed in the United States of America

No part of this publication may be reproduced or transmitted in any form or by any means, electronic or mechanical, including photocopy, recording, or any information storage or retrieval system now known or to be invented, without permission in writing from the publisher, except by a reviewer wishing to quote brief passages in connection with a review written for inclusion in a magazine, newspaper, or for broadcast.

Material in this publication may be utilized for workshop, audition, and classwork purposes without royalty consideration. If, however, the material is presented individually, or in total, before an audience where admission is charged, royalty payment is required. Contact publishers for applicable rates.

Dramaline Publications
36-851 Palm View Road
Rancho Mirage, CA 92270
Phone 619/770-6076 fax 619/770-4507

Cover art by John Sabel

This book is printed on 55# Glatfelter acid-free paper, a paper that meets the requirements of the American National Standard of Permanence of paper for printed library material.

CONTENTS

You Can't Beat Living Things   1
Nature Is Best   3
TV Programming Is Too Violent   5
Unemployment Is a Bad Thing   7
Shopping With Mom Is a Pain   9
Grouchy People Are Sad   11
Don't Judge a Book by Its Cover   13
Music Is a Matter of Personal Taste   15
Giving Is a Good Thing   17
Honesty Is the Best Policy   19
Grownups Don't Know How to Treat Kids   21
Running Away Isn't Easy   23
You Have to Give People a Chance   25
Imagining Shouldn't Be Just for Kids   27
Life Is Lonely Without a Pet   29
It's Important for Kids to Be Aware   31
Life is Precious   33
It's Nice to Have Family Nearby   35
Musical Taste Is a Personal Thing   37
Some Parents Push Their Kids Too Hard   39
Public School Has a Lot to Offer   41
It's Hard to Let Go of an Old Friend   43
Older Brothers and Sisters Are a Mystery   45
Parents are Overprotective Out of Love   47
Losing a Pet Is a Difficult Thing   49
Museums Aren't for Everyone   51
Visitations Can Be Hard on Kids   53
Parental Conflict Is Troubling   55
Who Needs Braces?   57
Sharing a Room Can Be a Problem   59

WORKSHEET

You Can't Beat Living Things

Yesterday my grandfather took my cousins and me to this weird place over on Main Street. It's called Animals of the World.

Animals of the World is this place where they stuff dead animals. All kinds of animals. They had a polar bear there that was as tall as the ceiling. It was really big. The man said that some hunter shot it up in Alaska.

They had a stuffed lion, a stuffed deer, a stuffed wolf, a stuffed antelope, a stuffed bear. They even had a stuffed penguin and a stuffed snake. They had every kind of animal you could think of. It was like going to a zoo full of stuffed stuff.

My grandfather said that sometimes hunters like to have the animals they shoot stuffed so they can stick them on their walls to show them off. He said that hunters are real proud of the animals they kill.

I thought the place was kind of creepy. I mean, with all these dead animals all over the place. And besides, why would anyone want to kill an animal? I think it's a whole lot neater having them alive.

WORKSHEET

_____

_____

_____

_____

_____

_____

_____

_____

Nature Is Best

It seems like every weekend my dad has to go and get out all of this garden stuff and go messing around in our yard. Every weekend he gets up real early and makes lots of noise. You can hear him a block away.

He has like this little tractor that he rides around on. And it makes all kinds of racket. It sounds like it's going to fall apart, or something. And Daddy looks real dorkey sitting on it, too—like this big oversized person riding on this toy. Sometimes I think he looks like an elephant riding a mouse. When I see him on it, I crack up.

He really loves to ride on his tractor, too. Yeah. Wow. You can tell from the smile he gets on his face. He buzzes around on it making all kinds of noise and running into trees and bushes and stuff. One time he almost ran over our dog. He goes kinda crazy when he's on the thing. He also has a Weed-Whacker and this thing that makes neat edges on the sidewalk and an electrical hedge trimmer. They're real noisy, too.

I wonder why it takes so much noise to take care of our grass and bushes and trees and stuff. Hey, like, they don't make any noise when they grow.

WORKSHEET

_____

_____

_____

_____

_____

_____

_____

_____

TV Programming Is Too Violent

I went into my brother Ron's room last night and he was watching a bunch of stupid junk on his TV. There were these people running around screaming and yelling and shooting each other. People were bleeding and falling down all over the place. It was like this war going on, or something.

Ron watches violent stuff like this all the time. He thinks people getting shot is cool. He and his friends even play these games where they are either soldiers or cops or far-out space creeps. This way they get to shoot each other. Sometimes I think Ronnie's brain is made out of pizza.

I like to watch the movies on the Disney Channel. They don't have anybody getting blown away in them. Last night they had this story about a girl and her grandmother; about how the girl went to live with her after her parents got divorced. It was really neat because when she went to live with her grandmother, she was sad and unhappy. But after she'd lived with her grandmother for a while, she started to be happy because she felt safe and loved.

It was a neat story. And nobody got shot. I think love is a whole lot neater than guns any day.

WORKSHEET

Unemployment Is a Bad Thing

My father used to work at the Tri-County Lumber Company over on the east side. He had a good job and he used to talk about it a lot. He was proud of his job.

Then, a few months ago, he goes and gets layed off because they didn't have enough business. It had something to do with the fact they couldn't cut down trees anymore. A whole bunch of people got layed off just like my dad. It really messed up the town.

Since daddy got layed off, he just sits around the house and watches TV. This is because he can't find anything to do. Mom says he's tried to find work everywhere. But nobody seems to want to hire anybody around here. There just isn't any work.

My mom and dad argue a lot now, too. Before, they never yelled at each other. When he was working, they got along good. Now, sometimes, they don't even talk to each other. Last night they had a fight and Daddy left and didn't come home till real late.

Since daddy lost his job, things are different. Our house used to be a happy place. Now it's kinda sad.

WORKSHEET

_____

_____

_____

_____

_____

_____

_____

_____

Sometimes Mom makes me go with her when she shops. I guess she thinks it's fun for me to hang around while she looks for stuff she doesn't need.

Sunday we went to the new mall over on the north side. It's so big that if you ever got lost in it, you'd never find your way out. And it was so crowded we had to park a mile away and walk across this big, huge lot. By the time we got to the mall I was already tired. And hot, too. Whew!

Mom said that we weren't going to stay very long. All she wanted to do was find a cute dress to wear to this party she was going to with Dad. She said she didn't have anything to wear. Nothing to wear? Is she kidding? You should see her closet. It's so full of junk she has trouble cramming stuff in.

She tried on a ton of dresses in a whole bunch of stores. It took all day. It was really boring. Sitting around watching my mom try to squeeze into clothes all day was awful. She broke two zippers.

I hate shopping. I'd rather stay home and mess around with my friends. Shopping is for old people who haven't got important things to do.

Maybe, if I'm lucky, Mom will get into the Home Shopping Network.

WORKSHEET

Grouchy People Are Sad

There are these people who live on the corner who never smile. They're always real grouchy. When I walk past their house I always smile at them if they're out in their yard. But they never smile back. They act like they don't see me. But they do. I know they do. And when they ignore me, it kinda hurts my feelings, you know.

My dad says that they've always been grouchy. He calls them "The Lemon People," because they're so sour all the time. And he says that I shouldn't get upset because they don't smile back. He says that I shouldn't let it hurt my feelings, that some people are just plain grumpy, that's all.

Even their kids don't smile. When I see them at school, they all have these real mean faces like they're mad, or something. Everyone stays away from them. I don't think they have any friends.

Know what? I shouldn't smile at them anymore. I mean, why should I be nice to a bunch of grouches? But . . . for some reason, I feel more sorry for them than anything else. So, hey! I'll just keep on smiling.

11

WORKSHEET

_____

_____

_____

_____

_____

_____

_____

_____

Don't Judge a Book by Its Cover

There is this new kid who just moved into our neighborhood. He moved here from New York City. He's real skinny and funny looking. My sister says he looks like a sick person. He also has this weird way of walking, kinda like he's going around in all directions at the same time. His name is Harold.

To look at him you'd think Harold was a double-dork. I mean, after all, if you'd ever see the way he looks and walks and acts, you'd think he was a dork, too—anybody would. 'Cause he gives the impression of a really weird, off-the-wall guy, you know.

Because he's weird, nobody was nice to him. And at first, because nobody was nice to him, I wasn't nice to him either. Until we got into the same class at school and I didn't have a clue what the teacher was talking about and the only kid who offered to help me was Harold. He was really neat. And super-smart.

Now Harold is my best friend. We mess around together all the time. And I don't ever think about the way he looks or walks anymore, because he's so nice and smart and so much fun.

From now on, I'm not going to treat people bad just because they're different, you know. I mean, hey! I'm different, too. We all are in this special way. And this is what makes us neat.

WORKSHEET

_____

_____

_____

_____

_____

_____

_____

_____

Music Is a Matter of Personal Taste

Whenever I play my CDs, my mom and dad tell me to turn the music down. Gee whiz! You can't play cool sounds real low. Everybody knows that. You have to listen to them super-loud to hear them right. But my parents say that the music my friends and I listen to is nothing but a bunch of noise. Shows what they know.

My mom listens to the real old people like Elvis and The Supremes and The Temptations, and people like that. She says that this is *real* music. To me it sounds like a whole bunch of sappy junk.

My dad listens to opera. Stuff that's a million years old. And he plays it louder than I do my music any day. Sometimes I can hear it way down the street. One time a neighbor called up and complained about it and the cops came and made him turn it down. They should have made him bust up all of his opera records, too, if you ask me. That way, I wouldn't have to listen to a bunch of dead people all screaming at the same time.

Hey, my music may be noisy, but at least the people playing it are still alive.

WORKSHEET

_____

_____

_____

_____

_____

_____

_____

_____

Giving Is a Good Thing

Over the weekend, my mom and dad and my brothers and sisters and I cleaned out our closets. We came up with a whole bunch of stuff we don't wear anymore. We filled up ten boxes. We went through everything and sorted it out and folded it up real neat. A lot of the stuff looked brand new. My mom said it was a shame. She said we had a lot more stuff than we ever needed. She said it was awful to buy a bunch of junk and then never wear it. Like she should talk. She filled up more boxes than anybody.

After we got the stuff all packed up, we loaded it into our van and took it down to this shelter place where there was a whole bunch of homeless people hanging out.

When we unloaded the stuff, you should have seen how they acted. You would have thought that we were bringing them the coolest stuff on earth, or something, instead of a pile of leftovers. One little kid was real happy when she tried on one of my old sweaters. You should have seen the look on her face. If was like she'd just won the lottery, or something. It was neat.

You know, I never realized how good giving could make you feel.

WORKSHEET

_____

_____

_____

_____

_____

_____

_____

_____

Honesty Is the Best Policy

My parents say that telling the truth is always the best thing to do. They say that truth is really important.

But, you know, sometimes telling the truth isn't so easy. Especially when you know that if you do you're going to get yelled at—or worse. And when my dad yells, he really yells. I mean, you can hear him all over the place. He sounds like a bear when he yells. It's scary. Wow!

The other day I had to stay in because I didn't help out around the house. *All day.* I hate being grounded. But when my friend came over and asked me to go for a Coke, I said, "Sure." I figured like nobody was at home, so who would know the difference, you know.

When my dad asked me that night at dinner if I'd stayed in, I said, "Yeah, sure." But my mom goes, "No you didn't, 'cause I saw you walking down Elm Street." Wow! I was trapped. Surrounded.

My dad yelled at me good and grounded me for a week. He said if I'd told the truth, he'd only grounded me for another day. Then he lectured me about truth till my meatloaf got cold.

The next time I goof, I'm telling the truth. I mean, I learned my lesson, you know. Dishonesty doesn't pay. And besides, who likes cold meatloaf?

WORKSHEET

_____

_____

_____

_____

_____

_____

_____

_____

I hate getting sick. 'Cause then I have to stay home and stay in bed and take all kinds of medicine. Even when I'm even a little bit sick, they make me take all kinds of crappy junk. They go bananas even if my temperature is one degree higher. You'd think I was dying, or something.

This is the reason, even when I feel really bad, that I try not to act it. 'Cause if I do, right away my mom goes feeling my head and shoving a thermometer in my mouth and calling up Grandma, who always recommends a laxative. You could cut your finger and she'd recommend a laxative. And then I have to go to bed and keep quiet. I can't even talk on the phone. I don't know what keeping quiet has to do with getting well. My mom gabs all the time when she's sick.

And when grownups get sick, they don't have to go to bed and take stinking medicine and pills as big as meatballs. They just keep on working and sneezing and coughing and blowing their noses and leaving used Kleenexes all over the place. They can be as sick as dogs without anyone shoving thermometers down their throats and telling them to be quiet.

I can't wait to be old. Then I can be as sick as I want and spread germs all over the place. Hey, when you're a grownup, even being sick is fun.

WORKSHEET

_____

_____

_____

_____

_____

_____

_____

_____

Running Away Isn't Easy

Yesterday I ran away because my mom and dad wouldn't let me stay up and watch my favorite TV shows. They were extra mean. Parents can be mean without even knowing they are, you know.

So, anyway, I got all my favorite stuff together and put it in this big Hefty Bag. Then I made myself a peanut butter and jelly sandwich. I took along a banana and a Pepsi, too. Hey, you can't go running away on an empty stomach.

I left right after Dad left for work and Mom was talking on the phone to Mrs. Harrison about cute shoes. When she's talking about cute stuff you could blow up the house and she wouldn't notice.

I think I chose a bad day to run away because it was really hot. Whew! And the farther I walked, the bag full of stuff seemed to get heavier and heavier. After about two hours, it seemed to weigh a ton. Then, alluva sudden, everything about me looked different and weird. It was like I was in this strange country, or something, and I was the only kid in the entire world. So, I sat down and ate the banana and thought about running away and how maybe it wasn't such a cool idea after all.

When I got back home, my mom was on the phone with Mrs. Ortega talking about cute dresses. I coulda gone to the moon for all she knew. So, I decided not to run away anymore. I mean, what's the point when nobody even notices?

WORKSHEET

_____

_____

_____

_____

_____

_____

_____

_____

_____

You Have to Give People a Chance

My mom died three years ago. She was really pretty and really nice. I loved her a whole bunch—more than anything. At first, without her around, I didn't think I'd ever be happy again. And my dad was real unhappy, too. He would just sit around looking like there was nothing in his eyes, nothing at all. Till he met Sally.

After he met Sally, he didn't seem sad anymore, and he didn't have time for me because he was always messing around with her. Then he goes and marries her, just like that, without even asking me, okay? Without even asking.

After Sally moved in, I stayed away from her as much as I could. I mean, after all, she wasn't my *real* mother. She was just . . . just somebody. Then one day I saw her crying. When I asked her what was wrong, she said that she was sorry for messing everything up. She said that she knew she could never take Mom's place, but that she loved Dad and was trying her best to make me like her. It was a real sad thing. Then she put her arms around me and we both cried. I never realized before that crying could be neat.

Everything's okay now. Sally and I get along really well and I'm glad she's here. She may not be my real mom, but she's my best friend.

WORKSHEET

_____

_____

_____

_____

_____

_____

_____

_____

Imagining Shouldn't Be Just for Kids

I think one of the neat things about being a kid is that kids can be all kinds of stuff by just imagining. You can be an astronaut, a nurse, a doctor, a ballerina, a movie star—anything. Hey, all you have to do is imagine. But grownups? Hey, it seems like they can't imagine anything, you know.

When I asked my Uncle Harry if he ever imagines he's somebody neat, he said that sometimes he imagines he's rich. But I told him I didn't mean rich. What I meant was, imagining he was like this famous detective, or something. He said this was silly. How could he be a detective when he was a plumber?

My grandmother said she hasn't time for imagining, that she's too busy trying to keep my grandfather from spending all their money on cars. She said that imagining is for kids.

But when I asked my mom, she said that imagining is good, that imagining is healthy. Just so long as you don't get carried away, that is. She said that sometimes she imagines that she's this beautiful princess living on this big island where all she has to do is lie around and have people wait on her. But then, she said, she has to come back to earth and do real stuff. Like the laundry.

WORKSHEET

Life Is Lonely Without a Pet

When we lived in our big house on Maple Street, I had a couple of really neat cats. They were around all the time and kept me company. But when my older brother went off to college and my sister moved out, my parents said we had too much room. How can you ever have too much room, anyway? Space is neat. Sometimes I think grownups work real hard at being lame. But, anyway, they said we had way too much room for just the three of us. So they went and sold the house and bought a condo.

The condo is brand new and has a swimming pool and tennis courts and a gym and all kinds of junk. But you can't have pets. So we had to leave the cats with our neighbors, the Williams. Like they have this big yard where the cats can run around and be free and go crazy.

I don't mind the condo, but I sure do miss having my cats. Even though I can visit them at the Williams' any time I want, it's not the same as having them around all the time. I mean, now I don't have anybody to talk to when nobody else will listen. And when I'm lonely I don't have anybody to play with. My cats were really cool and I miss them a lot. They were like special friends.

Hey! Living things are better than swimming pools and tennis courts any day of the week.

WORKSHEET

When we lived in the country, we used to play outside alone all of the time. We'd play tag and hide-and-seek and all kinds of neat games. And a lot of the time we played outside after it got dark.

But since we've moved to the city, we never get to play outside alone anymore. The only way we can go to the park or play outside is when either my mom or dad or some other grownups are around. They say it's too dangerous for us to be by ourselves. They say that we have to be extra careful now because there are people around who like to hurt little kids. Like this little girl who got kidnapped right out of her front yard last week. Somebody just came along and grabbed her, just like that. And so far they haven't found her. When I asked Mom why anyone would want to hurt a kid, she said that some people aren't nice, that some people are bad.

My mom always walks us to school now and comes to meet us after classes. Here it seems like we can't do anything alone. We don't have any freedom. It's sure not like when we lived in Colorado. There, we never ever thought about people getting us, we just played and had a good time.

Even though we'd rather be doing stuff like we used to, we understand that it's important to be careful when you have creeps around. The older you get, the more you realize a lot of stuff. And a lot of the stuff you realize makes you sad.

WORKSHEET

_____

_____

_____

_____

_____

_____

_____

_____

Life is Precious

It happened when I was crossing the street on my way home from school. I forgot to look both ways.

I don't remember the car hitting me. I don't remember anything. All I remember is waking up in the hospital with my mom and dad and grandparents and a whole bunch of doctors and nurses looking down at me. It was like really weird, you know. It was like waking up on the moon, or something.

I got my legs messed up pretty bad and had to be in casts for almost three months. And now I have to walk with crutches for a while. And I have to go to this therapy place every day, too.

At first I didn't think I could stand it. And I was in real bad pain. It was awful. And I was afraid, too. Afraid I'd never be able to walk again. I was *really* scared and down in the dumps.

Then I met this other kid in the hospital. He'd had to have his left leg removed. But he was like never in a bad mood. He was always real cheerful and never complained, or anything. And he made jokes all the time and made everyone laugh. He was really neat. He was special. And after I met him, and saw how brave he was, I didn't feel bad anymore. He made me realize that just being alive is the most important thing of all.

WORKSHEET

It's Nice to Have Family Nearby

My grandparents used to live across the street. And I used to see them all the time. It was really cool that I could go over to their house whenever I wanted to. I went there almost every day. And we used to do all kinds of stuff together, too. We had barbecues and dinners, and when there was a birthday, we always went to Grammy's and Grampy's. We were always getting together with them to do family stuff.

But after my grandfather retired from his job, he and my grandmother decided to move. They said they'd had it with the lousy weather. So they moved away last fall.

The day they left, all of the neighbors got together and we had this big farewell party. It was neat, but at the same time it was really sad, too. My dad made this speech and my mom cried.

After they left, things weren't as much fun as they used to be. Even though we visited them a couple of times, it still wasn't the same as when they were living across the street. I really missed them a lot. More than anything.

But guess what? Yesterday Mom told me that they've decided to move back just as soon as they sell their condo. Wow. I guess they miss me, too.

WORKSHEET

_____

_____

_____

_____

_____

_____

_____

_____

Musical Taste is a Personal Thing

I like music a lot. I mean, like rock and rap and stuff. But I really hate my music class. 'Cause all our music teacher—Mrs. Cashman—all she ever talks about is people like Beethoven and Mozart and a whole bunch of people that nobody cares about anymore. And she makes us sing all this old-timey stuff, too.

She plays the piano. And she sings, too. In this real loud, scratchy voice. And when she sings, she makes this weird face with her lips all puckered up. She looks just like a great big fish.

Yesterday, when we were singing this dumb piece of junk, Jimmy Clark sang in this real funny voice. He sounded just like a frog, or something. And Mrs. Cashman couldn't figure out who was doing it. She went ape. I thought she was going to freak for sure. Then he started making a face just like hers. I laughed so hard I almost swallowed my gum.

I wonder why Mrs. Cashman doesn't play regular music, some of the cool sounds like you hear on WXXY-FM instead of stuff that sounds like the junk they play at weddings. I guess she just doesn't know any of the new stuff. Or maybe Mozart is easier.

WORKSHEET

_____

_____

_____

_____

_____

_____

_____

_____

_____

Some Parents Push Their Kids Too Hard

I don't think grownups know how much kids get messed up when they're supposed to be super brains and super perfect. Hey, just because we're kids doesn't mean we don't feel pressure, too. My mom and dad are all the time talking about being stressed out, you know. They're always complaining about being nervous and having these headaches and stomachaches and stuff because of all the pressure they get on their jobs. Well, hey, kids feel the same way, too. Especially when we're expected to be perfect and act perfect and get perfect grades and be the best at everything.

Ya know, sometimes I'm so afraid of goofing up that it seems I can't do anything right. Because I know if I goof up, I'm gonna get yelled at and told I'm not trying hard enough. Like if I don't get all A's, my parents freak and scream and get crazy. Hey, I see them goof up all the time. If I was grading them on the stuff they do, I'd give them a D.

I wish grownups would give us kids a break. Hey, nobody's perfect. They must think we're robots here, or something. I just wish they'd relax and not expect so much of us. I wish they'd chill out.

WORKSHEET

_____

_____

_____

_____

_____

_____

_____

_____

Public School Has a Lot to Offer

I used to be in this private school. It was over in the north end of town. It was a quiet place and not crowded and we had all kinds of equipment. Our classes were pretty small—maybe fifteen or twenty kids. We got lots of attention. We wore uniforms, too. We all dressed alike.

Then my dad had some kind of trouble with his business and alluva sudden we didn't have money coming in like we used to. So, they told me that I had to go into a public school because they couldn't afford to keep me in a private one anymore. Boy, was I ever bummed. I mean, only stupid jerks go to public schools, right?

At first I really hated it. I guess maybe because I wanted to, you know. But after I made a few friends and got to know the teachers and stuff, it was no big deal. And I found out that the kids weren't so stupid after all. No way. In fact, they were doing stuff a whole lot harder than we ever did in private school. And even though the classes are bigger, I'm still learning a lot because the teachers are real concerned and take a lot of time with everybody. They seem to really care.

I've gotten to like my new school better than my old one. The kids are more down to earth and a lot more friendly. And, oh yeah, now I get to wear cool clothes.

WORKSHEET

_____

_____

_____

_____

_____

_____

_____

_____

It's Hard to Let Go of an Old Friend

I used to drag this crappy, old, fuzzy stuffed dog around with me all the time. I called him Sam. I took him with me everywhere. Sam was all grubby and his ears were off to the point where he looked like a big mouse. But he was like a special friend, or something, you know. I used to talk to him and everything. I'd had Sam since I was a little kid.

My mom and dad kept telling me that I was too old for such stuff. That kids my age didn't go around dragging an old toy. They said it was childish.

Lots of time they'd hide Sam and say he must have gotten misplaced or thrown out by accident, or something. They would make up all kinds of stories. But I knew better. And I always found him and put him back on my bed. Hey, kids can find anything. Especially when they're not supposed to, you know.

Then, one time, when we went on vacation, I forgot to take Sam along. When I found out, I went bananas and screamed and kicked the seats of the car till my dad gave me one of his looks. The kind of look that says, "One more peep and you're history." So I shut up fast. And that did it. By the time we got back from our trip, I didn't need Sam anymore.

I still have him, though. He's up in the top of my closet. When Dad asks me why I keep him, I tell him I don't really know. I guess for the same reason he still has his old Teddy bear.

WORKSHEET

_____

_____

_____

_____

_____

_____

_____

_____

My brother and sister are a lot older than me. Dan is fifteen and Julie is almost seventeen. And they're all the time yelling at me and calling me a dweeb.

Dan runs around with a bunch of dorks. A bunch of guys who think they're super-cool. Hey, if they only knew. What they are is a bunch of stuck-up jerks. They just walk in the house without knocking and eat up everything and turn off the TV program I'm watching like I'm not even in the room. Wow. What a bunch of goons.

And Julie acts like she's this princess, or queen, or something. She's all the time looking into the mirror and messing with her face and hair and stuff. She wears so much makeup you'd think she'd stuck her head in a barrel of flour. And she's on the phone twenty-four hours a day talking about cute boys and cute shoes and cute clothes. Cute, cute, cute . . .

They treat me like I'm nothing, you know. Like I'm a piece of furniture, or something. So yesterday, when they did what they did, I couldn't believe it, you know. When this big kid pushed me around, they went and told him if he ever touched me again, they'd waste him. Hey, and I thought they hated me.

Know what? Maybe they don't think I'm such a dweeb after all.

WORKSHEET

_____

_____

_____

_____

_____

_____

_____

_____

Parents are Overprotective Out of Love

It seems like I can't do anything. Because it seems like everything I do is going to get me hurt or into some kind of trouble. My mom's always yelling stuff like: "Don't put money in your mouth!" "Don't run with scissors!" "Don't go too close to the edge!" "Don't leave the yard alone!" "Don't talk to strangers!" "Don't eat so fast, you'll get sick!" "Don't pet that animal, you don't know where it's been." Don't! Don't! Don't! My mom is full of don'ts. Wow. I mean, if I listened to all the stuff she told me not to do, I wouldn't be able to move. I'd have to stay in bed all day. She even yelled at me for eating my French fries too fast. Like there's this speed limit on French fries, or something? Hey, nobody can eat French fries slow—nobody.

Sometimes I think my mom's a worry wart. Besides, all the stuff she warns me about I already know. I mean, everybody knows better than to talk to strangers.

When I asked my dad about it and he said Mom doesn't mean anything by it, it's just that she loves me. Then he goes, "Don't fidget while I'm talking to you!"

My dad's full of don'ts, too.

47

WORKSHEET

_____

_____

_____

_____

_____

_____

_____

_____

Losing a Pet Is a Difficult Thing

We'd had Happy ever since I was a little kid. We got him from the pound. He wasn't a fancy, high-class dog, he was just a dog. But he was really smart. And friendly. Happy liked everyone.

Every morning when I left for school, he would stand in the door and watch me till I was out of sight. And every night he'd run to meet me when I came home. He'd run all the way down the block. Happy was a cool dog. A lot of times I liked him better than people.

Last month, Happy ran out into the street and got hit by a car. It wasn't the driver's fault. Happy ran out to meet my dad and the guy couldn't stop. But Happy got hurt bad. They had to put his rear legs in casts.

For a few days, Happy seemed to be okay. Then he started acting strange and began whining and stuff. When we took him back to the vet, he told us that Happy had internal injuries and was in a lot of pain and that he wasn't going to get well. So, they put him to sleep.

Things are pretty quiet around here without Happy. We all miss him a lot. He was like a member of the family.

WORKSHEET

_____

_____

_____

_____

_____

_____

_____

_____

Museums Aren't for Everyone

This week we had a field trip to the museum. My mom said it would be good for me. She kidding? How can a museum be good for you? Exercise is good for you, proper food's good for you, lots of sleep. . . . But a museum . . .?

The place was really far out. Weird. It looked like where the Addams Family lives. Inside it was worse. One room was full of a bunch of naked statues and a bunch of junk that looked like when I knock over my Legos. And there were tons of paintings of naked people by old-time Dutch guys. And another room was full of these paintings that were nothing but lines and circles and squares and stuff. One looked like stepped-on pizza. And *it* was worth a hundred thousand dollars. Go figure.

We had this guide who tried to explain what the junk meant. But what she said didn't make any sense to anybody. And she told us this stupid story about like this guy who whacked off his ear. From the looks of his stuff, he must have used if for a paint brush.

When Mom asked me what I thought, I said most of the stuff looked like when our cat barfs.

WORKSHEET

_____

_____

_____

_____

_____

_____

_____

_____

Visitations Can Be Hard on Kids

But I don't wanna go up to Dad's, Mom, I wanna stay home with you. . . . 'Cause every time I go, he just sits around all weekend and won't do anything. Hey, I know I'm supposed to go every other week. But I don't care. I'm *not* going! I'd rather die than hang around up there. The last time, all we did was sit around in his stupid little apartment and watch TV. And we hardly even talked. It was awful. You don't know. You don't have to be there.

And he argues with me all of the time. And he finds fault with me, picks on me like crazy for every little thing. He says I watch too much TV. What else am I going to do? And he complains about me not getting better grades and for not exercising and not . . . you name it, I can't do anything right.

Look, I don't care, I'm not going! You can't make me. Nobody has any right to make someone do something they hate. . . . I know he's my father. So what? If you think he's so neat, why'd you divorce him? Huh? I'll tell you why. Because he's a pain, that's why. Because he hasn't got anything good for anybody.

When people get divorced, they don't think about the kids, all they think about is themselves and being free. Well, what about kids' freedom? Why do they have to be the ones who get pushed around? Does anybody *ever* think about the kids?

WORKSHEET

_____

_____

_____

_____

_____

_____

_____

_____

Parental Conflict Is Troubling

Sometimes my mom and dad get into these terrible arguments. They yell and scream at each other so loud you can hear them all over the place. It's awful.

Most of the time, though, they're nice to each other. Most of the time, things are okay. And it's nice when nobody's yelling. I hate yelling. Yelling's bad news.

I don't know why they argue. When I try to think why they do, I can never think of a good reason. It just seems like one minute everything's okay, and then the next . . . then they're screaming and yelling. I don't even think that *they* know why they're arguing.

Sometimes, after they argue, they don't speak to each other for hours. Last weekend they didn't speak for two days. I hate it when they don't talk. It gives me the creeps. I think not speaking is not only stupid, it's also kinda sick, you know. I think I hate it more when they're not speaking than when they're arguing. When they're arguing, at least they're doing *something*.

Kids argue sometimes, too. But they usually make up right away and it's all over. But grownups don't seem to get over their arguments so easy. And they argue about the same old stuff over and over again.

You know, sometimes grownups don't act as grown up as kids.

WORKSHEET

Who Needs Braces?

When they told me I had to get braces, I thought, No problem. Hey, it was going to be really neat. I mean, like almost everybody has braces, you know. All the kids. So I thought getting braces was gonna be cool.

I asked the orthodontist for plastic. I thought plastic would look a whole lot better than a mouthful of metal. And I had him give me red, white, and blue rubber bands. I wanted to look patriotic.

But you know what? Braces aren't cool, they're ugly and painful. And just when you start kinda feeling good, you have to go back in and they tighten up the rubber bands. Then the pain starts up all over again. I think the dental goons love the pain part.

And braces look awful. It's like you've always got a mouthful of mashed potatoes, or something. Gross. And you have to watch what you eat, too. Forget about corn-on-the-cob and candy and anything with sugar. And you have to brush all the time and floss and rinse your mouth and take special care of your teeth.

Boy, was I ever wrong about braces. They're nothing but a big pain in the face. And after a while they aren't cool, they're embarrassing. When I laugh, I put my hand over my mouth. I *hate* braces. I'd have them taken off, but I don't wanna grow up looking like a beaver.

WORKSHEET

_____

_____

_____

_____

_____

_____

_____

_____

Sharing a Room Can Be a Problem

I share a room with my sister (brother). And she's (he's) a real slob. She (he) throws her (his) stupid junk all over the place. And as hard as I try to keep my side neat, she (he) can mess it up in five minutes. She's (he's) the only person I know who can trash a room by just walking through it.

Yesterday she (he) threw her (his) dirty clothes all over my bed and trashed my dresser with her (his) stupid stuff. I flipped. I told her (him) she (he) had to stay on her (his) side of the room from now on. So we decided to divide our room in half.

I told her (him) that her (his) half would go from the end of the dresser to the lamp. But she (he) said, "No way! You're cheating. My half starts at the middle of the room and goes to the table." She's (he's) such a greedy jerk. So I go, "Forget it. We'll measure." So I got Dad's tape measure and figured out exactly one half of the room and marked it off with red thumb tacks.

Now we have our own separate sides. And boy, can you ever tell the difference. My side is always real neat and hers (his) is always totally sloppy with dirty clothes and papers and dried up plates of food and junk. My sister (brother) is a mess.

It's no wonder her (his) favorite animal is a pig.

ORDER DIRECT

MONOLOGUES THEY HAVEN'T HEARD, Karshner. Speeches for men and women. $9.95.
MORE MONOLOGUES HAVEN'T HEARD, Karshner. More living-language speeches. $9.95.
FOR WOMEN: MONOLOGUES THEY HAVEN'T HEARD, Pomerance. $8.95.
MONOLOGUES for KIDS, Roddy. 28 wonderful speeches for boys and girls. $8.95.
MORE MONOLOGUES for KIDS, Roddy. More great speeches for boys and girls. $8.95.
SCENES for KIDS, Roddy. 30 scenes for girls and boys. $8.95.
MONOLOGUES for TEENAGERS, Karshner. Contemporary teen speeches. $9.95.
SCENES for TEENAGERS, Karshner. Scenes for today's teen boys and girls. $9.95.
HIGH-SCHOOL MONOLOGUES THEY HAVEN'T HEARD, Karshner. $8.95.
MONOLOGUES from the CLASSICS, ed. Karshner. $8.95.
SHAKESPEARE'S MONOLOGUES THEY HAVEN'T HEARD, ed. Dotterer. $8.95.
MONOLOGUES from CHEKHOV, trans. Cartwright. $8.95.
MONOLOGUES from GEORGE BERNARD SHAW, ed. Michaels. $7.95.
MONOLOGUES from OSCAR WILDE, ed. Michaels. $7.95.
WOMAN, Pomerance. Monologues for actresses. $8.95.
MODERN SCENES for WOMEN, Pomerance. Scenes for today's actresses. $7.95.
MONOLOGUES from MOLIERE, trans. Dotterer. $9.95.
SHAKESPEARE'S MONOLOGUES for WOMEN, ed. Dotterer. $8.95.
DIALECT MONOLOGUES, Karshner/Stern. 13 essential dialects applied to contemporary monologues. Book and cassette tape. $19.95.
YOU SAID a MOUTHFUL, Karshner. Tongue twisters galore. $8.95.
TEENAGE MOUTH, Karshner. Modern monologues for young men and women. $8.95.
SHAKESPEARE'S LADIES, ed. Dotterer. $7.95.
BETH HENLEY: MONOLOGUES for WOMEN, Henley. *Crimes of the Heart*, others. $8.95.
CITY WOMEN, Smith. 20 powerful, urban monologues. Great audition pieces. $7.95.
KIDS' STUFF, Roddy. 30 great audition pieces for children. $9.95.
KNAVES, KNIGHTS, and KINGS, ed. Dotterer. Shakespeare's speeches for men. $8.95.
DIALECT MONOLOGUES, VOL. II, Karshner/Stern. 14 more important dialects. Farsi, Afrikaans, Asian Indian, etc. Book and cassette tape. $19.95.
RED LICORICE, Tippit. 31 great scene-monologues for preteens. $8.95.
MODERN MONOLOGUES for MODERN KIDS, Mauro. $8.95.
A WOMAN SPEAKS: WOMEN FAMOUS, INFAMOUS and UNKNOWN, ed. Cosentino. $9.95.
FITTING IN. Monologues for kids, Mauro. $8.95.
VOICES. Speeches from writings of famous women, ed. Cosentino. $9.95.
FOR WOMEN: MORE MONOLOGUES THEY HAVEN'T HEARD, Pomerance. $8.95.
NEIL SIMON MONOLOGUES. From the plays of America's foremost playwright. $12.95.
CLASSIC MOUTH, ed. Cosentino. Speeches for kids from famous literature. $8.95.
POCKET MONOLOGUES for WOMEN, Pomerance. 30 modern speeches. $9.95.
WHEN KIDS ACHIEVE, Mauro. Positive monologues for preteen boys and girls. $8.95.
FOR WOMEN: POCKET MONOLOGUES from SHAKESPEARE, Dotterer. $8.95
MONOLOGUES for TEENAGE GIRLS, Pomerance. $8.95.
POCKET MONOLOGUES for MEN, Karshner. $8.95.
COLD READING and HOW to BE GOOD at IT. Hoffman. $9.95.
POCKET MONOLOGUES: WORKING-CLASS CHARACTERS FOR WOMEN, Pomerance. $8.95.
MORE MONOLOGUES FOR TEENAGERS, Karshner. $8.95.

Send your check or money order (no cash or COD) plus handling charges of $4.00 for the first book and $1.50 for each additional book. California residents add 8.25 % tax. Send your order to: Dramaline Publications, 36-851 Palm View Road, Rancho Mirage, California 92270-2417.